Womonster

Womonster

poems by

Olivia Cronk

Tarpaulin Sky Press
Chicago, IL
Saxtons River, VT
2020

Womonster
© 2020 Olivia Cronk
ISBN-13: 978-1-939460-22-6
Printed and bound in the USA.

Cover art by Michael Bramford, based on an image of Emily Greenquist from *ROMERO*, a docu-soap-opera-fantasy by Greenquist and Cronk.

Book design by Meg Forajter & Christian Peet.

Tarpaulin Sky Press
PO Box 189
Grafton, VT 05146
tarpaulinsky.com

For more information on Tarpaulin Sky Press trade paperback and hand-bound editions, as well as information regarding distribution, personal orders, and catalogue requests, please visit our website at tarpaulinsky.com.

CONTENTS

INTERRO-PORN

(for a split voice)
(with a Françoise Hardy album)

whose mouth

and quite plainly understood that it wasn't really that she preferred her gold hoop earrings to the opal studs; rather, it was a question of seasons and moods and anyway Drusilla wouldn't notice and anyway *heat*—the vexing heat of a city's summer: under the sway, on the Left Bank, across the street from, in front of the corner store, the subway tunnel, the line at the bank, the elegant garden-pause in the boulevard, Midwestern, Atlantic, intercontinental, European tourist plaza-esque, Mexico City cathedral, street hollerings, playground, squinting into the leafy sketch of city time, crumbled comics page, fish smell, and on and on. So she wore a green shirtdress. So she was going downtown to pay a ticket. So she ARE YOU (SHE) READING A NOVEL? DOES IT PLEASE YOU? ARE YOU SIPPING YOUR WATER?

I want my husband to come home in the rain
I want my husband to come home in the rain
And then be the INTERROGATOR

A tide of gestures is a clock. DID YOU READ "COCK"? Excise that.

I want my husband to come in the rain

nor the Giorgio de Chirico alley
nor thistle-pox-thigh-skin
showing up in the bedroom mirror
nor my daughter nor filming it the picture we made on no budget Back Then
I Was in
the Buttered Hands
of a Sweetheart

I
am vinyl
I jelly I
don't recall that address.

My *boyfriend*

picked me up
when he got off.
We drank lots and right now even when I try to remember
it's all TV-ish
when he got off.

Is that light necessary?
I'm sure I don't know what you mean

secretly remembering it all
in the poodle nest

they were *handsomely* paid for their milks

& licking the skin into place

Oh a little jack setting of poisoned meat is all a lady needs.

Toss in a stiff light bulb a soiled bed—
She looks into the camera like spreading a disease

How I am unnecessarily secretive, a kind of clannish posture inherited from my
mother, the paranoid & provincial stench on us.

My brother and I look askance at anyone who freely offers information.

How this tick
is all the best remembering in ALL the best songs.

To be perfectly frank, I'm mostly interested in the Tsar's daughters' farewell bedroom

its midday light

or spiky flowers growing on a tiger's back

or a dress opening up
to a delightful horde
of frightened spiritualists

   having hidden for a decade under the time-warp of a sideboard in the dusty
   crystal rose Henry James parlor their eyes bloody snails on a TV screen, they
   holler and

it is eternal—

WHY CHOOSE
TO *SMOOTHE MY WOMEN INTO OUTFITS?*

I CHOOSE IT.

As a girl, I cut women from my grandmother's catalogs (mostly plus-sized
clothing for work and vacation) and made paper dolls. When I ran out of those, I
drew pictures of women with perms, in office outfits and in commuter gymshoes
over bobby socks and pantyhose. I drew women with bangles, can still remember
perfecting the line around a wrist, a trick I now do for my daughter, when she asks
to be drawn as a princess.

DID YOU EVER tell Daddy about X making a pass at you after you and he
after you went and he

walking us kids to school?
What WOULD he have done?

trouser-socks from the pharmacy aisles lady lady eighties
cotton blouses a dresser drawer a drawer with sachets and
Suave shampoo
apple straw
berry watermelon popsicle and the sticky line of hair
coming out to the backyard after a shower summer slick
kiddie pool the marks of the lawn chair on the backs of thighs and beer cans
and the hose

Well did you?

Brittney-Spears-style-handgun-dildo-anti-morality transcendentalism?

Was that what you came for?
But now that you've set that buzzing light bulb,

and the choice-ee concerns about class and taste
and you unfold your hand to a rash of petty scandals and
you're like pow I got you and thick it is in here
thick indeed.

You're dead meat baby.
You're not gonna kill the Internet, and you already missed your chance to sleaze
up your thirties.

I'm sure I don't know what you mean
but that choke of diamonds
is certainly sweetening the deal.

DID YOU WATCH THE RIHANNA VIDEO TO RIP OFF HER STYLE?
AND A FLEETWOOD MAC, TOO??? WHERE DO YOUR PLEASURE,
YOUR THIEVING END?

DID YOU ever get into the stagnant bath of a real confession? Slip inside into
living in a body as a site of decadent filth?

Too late for it to be acceptable, I shit my pants out of an inability to leave my
playing. I was addicted to the pretending, sitting in front of my dollhouse, fastened
to it—and then this other, confluent, bizarre, easy transgression,
my white underpants stuck to me as a document of my hedonism.
I would simply wrap them in paper and throw them away.

What next thing will give me pleasure?

Once I have it, I imagine it and settle its dolly stage around me.
I wait for it in utter melancholy I dress for it.

But then
it is nothing at all.
It is just
nothing.
An irritating flight. An utter bore of an evening.
Flashy film-files flipped up/on: Charlotte Gainsbourg walks downtown
with the lady from *I Dream of Jeannie*: YES MASTER. YOU CAN
GO YOUR OWN WAY.

and anyway Drusilla
did you find
my husband in the rain

did you clench your little ring'ed fingers into a bite-fist
and hold it
up to your jaw

and had you
just cut a record
and
you were were you
wearing a low hat on the rainy street
a jug of wine in the trunk

while I was in the forest's hard bruising tooth,

while I was in the snap of it letting loose on me
WHERE THE FUCK
WERE YOU?
did one finger climb out of the fist and summon my man to a railroad room yes

I won't listen anymore to the hissed up tapes of the INTERROGATOR
nor to the Friday train with its loads of wormed bodies
nor the tidy lunch at half past noon nor the flooded patio

the mashed sound of these things disgusts me when I am filming in red

I come to
in the restaurant
and I am mid-conversation in a booth in a discotheque at a handsome mobster's dinner
Joe Adonis Joe with the slick cut of suit and a geometric tie a silver blow dryer at home
I
in a white dress in wet mauve eyeshadow
and when finally everyone finally bleeds onto the carpet,
I am filming it RED I am disgusted

HAVE YOU EVER BEEN IN TROUBLE BEFORE?
CAN WE GET YOU A BIT OF COFFEE?

WHAT WAS THE GATE?

It was a narrow gaze of phallic facial spikes as I rode my bike to work.

So I went to the cemetery and I went to the river
and circled round and counted more than one moon. An alien ball
zipped me to the land.
I felt intense devastation.

And then, so the guide said, I was prepared to consume the entry.

I minted my own hands. I peered through the glass
and looked for Drusilla or Giselle or Griselda.

You have to understand that I was not looking for hellbreed nor for pussycat cashmere.
I was just caught at the gate
with all the other poisons.

WHAT ABOUT ALL THOSE VICTORIAN BOY FACES IN THE SNOW?

Yeah yeah yeah.

By the time
the awkward social encounter becomes pleasing embroidery
by the time you get to Phoenix
on the self
the self I wish to manufacture, curate, I don't know.
& I don't know.
What about all those boy faces?

Watercolor maps, French songs, wintery hair that lays badly.

I'd like to lead a small tour of people to a small hilltop to
over a look to
a vile dropping planet
a crashing scene to a body with no skin and
it rightly zipped into a casino bathrobe
with dollars printed all over it
and the blood fours prints fouring on the carpet

but all of this happening under my sweeping care, AND THE TOUR GROUP
(WHAT OF THE TOUR GROUP?) they would all see something horrible
horrendous

womonster
licking at HER screams

and then the group would just be screaming and crying, "What is it
"What is it

heard the sudden thud of a blow, heard Griselda felt Drusilla nearby. Giselle and Barbara Eden now laughing on the balcony. Griselda was seeing her ruby ring reflected in the glass sliding door and seeing it all so terrible feeling awful bad in her knee-length cotton hosiery and black high heels and just the bad bad feelings of why did she get so high the good first feeling of weed gone now and now too much fear. And you know

that almost all girls

delight in the jeweled ankle straps just put them on Griselda WHEN WILL YOU?

I demanded my old man
be his own forecast of lace on the bridge in fog
a soft kind of shame
shame face
shame face caught in the rearview mirror

It was a rather vilifying possession of his body a contaminated skull mirror crack
The   being poured into time
And if YOU were in the room, what question would you ask us what ask say and
always reading a book just to stand up and die in village years

IN WHAT SELF-SWALLOWING HOLE DO YOU, NOW?

TO WHOM AM I NOW SPEAKING?
WHERE IS THE INTERROGATOR?
FOR WHOM DO YOU SPEAK?

WHOSE MOUTH DOES WEAR THESE STILLETO CHARMERS, HUH?

I hate for others to see my face as it appears in a mirror.

Did YOU EVER WATCH the 1991 exorcism on *20/20*?
My brother and I shrieked with laughter and thrill, good Catholics.
When I think of voices on a page, I sometimes think of the girl on the screen,
but more often I think of our replaying/re-enacting the television event,

a private, giddy theater, a script to which only we had access,

while walking to school. We did this many days in a row.

The information moving across different media. Squirming in a cord, squirming
into our gaze. Squirming through holes in time and memory. ARE YOU
LISTENING TO THE FRANÇOISE HARDY ALBUM RIGHT NOW?

I am starting to worry that my fashion observations are surveillance.

BUT NOW WE'RE IN DANGER OF READING THE DEAR JOHN
AHEAD OF THE CHARACTER
OH TRICKY MINXY CINEMA
CINEMA CAN DO ALL EYES
CAN SEE ALL THE DAMN WOMEN
SUCKING ON ALL THE FOUCAULDIAN OPERATORS

& I have more acute observation skills than do you
& I understand the game is played in costume.

But then.
Summer.

I was a high-rise lifeguard in a cute bikini and pale blue nail polish.
I mean, seriously. This part is real: I was slender and seventeen and working a
pool on top of a residential high-rise in Chicago's Gold Coast neighborhood.

I spent my days thusly:
scrub the deck with bleach for two hours in the morning, take a water break, put
my uniform shirt back on over my bikini, check the chlorine, greet and watch
the daily swimmers (rich people with their weekday mornings free —one old
man, an anesthesiologist at Northwestern, who seemed smitten), eat lunch, sit
on the mostly empty pool deck

and read about/drown in tender-night Zelda and the rest of them.
Oh my blue nail polish, my long legs, if you coulda seen it. The French Riviera.
The gin & fights & all of it.
I was teetering over Lake Michigan, atop this silvery phallus of a building.
On top of this for real shit.

Moms who go to the grocery store in a t-shirt and jeans and big earrings like
moms who go after work in nylons and gymshoes work clothes uniforms like
moms who buy Diet Rite like moms

too many moms to know
my old contemptuous attitudes gone now

poisoned bloody mary
tipped over house plant
the huge imperialist view over a body of water

Remember how people on TV used to get hit over the head with flower vases?
And fall down in the foyer?

I was at the movies then.

If you just pass me my purse I am absolutely certain I can produce a ticket.

The only strange thing about that day was that I swear to god I saw an old-timey-demon-face peeking up over the carpet-block-slide-thing at the back of the movie lobby, but then when I asked Drusilla—

This is straight up pointillism and you know it.
IS THIS POINTILLISM?

DO YOU RECOGNIZE THIS PIPE? IS THIS BAG YOURS? THIS BLOODY BRA? IS THIS POINTILLISM?

I should bring you to my circle of witch trees

and electronic drumming machines lifting your woolen skirt
and devout as you are little mommy you know
and a limp a cold sore
a socially ill at ease grimace
does not register on video not at all

and you laid laden with lizard brooches and howling like no mother I ever seen.

I'm still glad of the play on
in which event
is
bottom poetry.
That's my place & I know it.

She could see the graphs laid right over the room then
in air in concepts in quiet smoke trees in slow-mo out the window smoke
shake no no must get the lawyer in here.

WHEN YOU STEPPED ONTO YOUR BUS, WERE YOU PARANOID?

Ma, if you read the tabloids about my being in the crime's pocket, my eyeliner
smeared to graveyard-sex and my trunk fulla bad bad things, would you call me
up & feign surprise? Ma, how does this hat look? Miss Otis Regrets?

Goddammit I want a slowly narrated scene of an empress and then some kind of betrayal and then Instagram eyebrows peeking out from under shiny bangs and a piece of poisoned glass and an honest-to-god magical demon.

I used to think only big earrings and then only dark eye makeup and then filth and then country-music-cuteness or good curation of the livingroom trinkets. I don't give a shit about cleanliness, but tidiness for the purpose of unseen display now that is something I appreciate.

I'll sweep the room.
No, it's better if it's a room with carpeting to vacuum: blue, pastel: crystaleeny figurinees on a brassy edge. THIS IS NOT MY HOUSE. This is how I would set a room to make a porno. I vacuum all morning, crank up the AC, put out a few cherry candies and some vodka-lemonade jobbies, and invite the cast to relax.

The empress barricades the house in which the dead emperor remains. Everyone is putting on too much lipstick. A torn paper silhouette taped to the wall comes loose in the excess of luscious humidity. You shall say the dentist is here double canines and two heads emerging from a cornucopia. Tend to this. With your mouth.

Every script that comes
cross desk

I think I've already filmed this one I've already done this
but no it's I've already ripped this off.

WHAT ARE YOUR TRICKS?
CAN I STEAL THEM?

I want my women to be just a clump of regular girls and at the same time,

hear me out sweetie, face up and gone dead and open
it's so fucking familiar it's absolutely labored

to have the distinctive characteristics of the actual women I adore and seek to emulate
and for whom my affection and aesthetic appreciation are completely bound—

near and far.
So you see

that is why

I must
simply must
dress them in green capelets
and send them to a sexy jail
and film them opening letters opening again and
open snappy little letter openers brutal tear-offs with clumsy hands and clever
teeth shanking a pull-tab.
And then lights dim, good night, little ones. Faretheewell my swilly switchboard.

You gotta ask yourself about breathing into theater,
simply sighing the room into pretend

Then you ask about the script there is so much ambiguity how do the incantations
work with this necktie this rubber lead this boa this saying over
while saying it   how can I make the VOICE SPLIT THAT WAY?
HOW DOES A VOICE WORK WHEN IT'S MADE OF SO MUCH
RIPPED OFF SHIT? WHEN I AM READING AM I?

DOES THE VOICE SPLIT THAT WAY?

Tell the performers to drink right from the room.
A reminder people look alive it's an interrogation room it's a funeral it's
shit-shiny chrome and powdered hounds

To kill what I kill is fine.
HAVE YOU EVER BEFORE SEEN THIS GOLD PEACOCK BROOCH?
"Have you ever seen this gold peacock brooch?" Have I?

Have I ever been caught with the likes of you

sniffing out my dog and my red bracelet? Am I wearing a pilled sweater?

There's nothing in here for me that is ghastly enough for me.

DID YOU WEAR THIS BROOCH
WEAR IT, AS YOU, UNDER THE BRIDGE?

WERE YOU WAITING AND SEEPING AND SEETHING?

I waited tables at a Nepalese place in a college town. The owner's mother told us to drink water every hour and light incense upstairs and make the salad dressing more carefully: Peel Garlic (instead of Smoke Cigarettes in the Gangway).

A bunch of us girls in black blouses and long white aprons. We stashed our winter boots, swapped out for stylish clogs, in the storage closet. Some girls changed there into bar outfits, showing off hot pink bras and sloppy tattoos; not I. My boyfriend picked me up when he got off of work. We drank lots and right now even when I try to remember it's all TV-ish.

I took my child to some rich people's front yard & pained around in my I am seriously not joking in a blouse I used to wear in high school, but it's back in.

A whole lotta stuff about women and yards and drunk scenes. This was not my ma. She was straight. She is straight. She did plenty a wild things
plenty a early times
but stopped.

Back then, my ma bleached her armpit hair, wore a black three-piece suit, wore eyelet lace, a rainbow turtleneck, a scowl, wintertime capes; now, black petal pushers and bright t-shirts, sensible sandals, large jewelry, sometimes loud red lips.

And when my daughter my mother necks her little face out the front windows
of our apartment and hollers at the whole block, I see it is Barbara fucking Eden
herself who yanks her back in

to watch the teevee

They both know I'm busy with the film: a garden scene, a hand turning into
a chain, Giselle and Drusilla at it again, red lace on the boots getting simply
drowned in fake snow/semen/powdered hounds, what have you.

I am intimate as earrings with these assholes and that's not changing any time soon.

The pinning of time to time to day to year,
as layers laced through
for a fantasy-outfit-day.

No.
You don't know shit.

Get out of the goddamn theater-piece. Leave it behind.

READER, THIS BOOK SEEKS TO ASK:

WHY DO I/YOU HOW DO I/YOU SIMULTANEOUSLY ABHOR AND
LUXURIATE IN NARRATIVE & MEMOIR?

WHAT SEX IS PSYCHEDELIA IS SEX, THE FAILINGS OF MEMORY?

WHAT NOW
YOUR DISGUST AND YOUR GAWK?

It is her divinely frantic leather plight.

It is this:
go into each room, sniff out the dirty princess dress, find it stuffed into a leaky corner.

Sniff it out.

Giselle WILL get her ass beat down.

She came to town. She came
all over the neighborhood. Giselle
gnawed an apple and wore a spiky collar & listen up

don't come near my man don't whistle his tune he's got no ears for it now

WHAT DID YOUR MOTHER WEAR ON MONDAY?

who's chirping yer hand?

(fashion reportage wallpaper theater)

Griselda
wants it

My mother always made her eyebrows on a Maybelline brow pencil
She rarely left the house without mascara

Griselda says she says it while lounging on her bed and licking her fingers to
deal with magazine pages and she says it so bad somehow she is so so bad

I remember watching in fascination as she separated her lashes with a safety pin to
break up the clumps

When we come back to Griselda, she is all mint lozenges &
ironing the detachable lace edges of her shams.

My mother had a blue silk kimono bathrobe, a dragon,

Griselda Giselle scream together in the dawn-y light
Griselda Giselle in denim jumpers
wearing nothing but *expired Charlie perfume*

Who are Griselda Giselle on me leaking on me?

Griselda
Giselle
wanted on the set
want you to want them to want you to catch their ankle bones in your teeth
inside of the sliver of hot fake moon
here ladies here
recline here in the little golden light of sucking on,

(Stage whisper.)
Always a white nightgown. Long cotton.
Lacy top part like Little House on the Prairie.
Sometimes a ruffle at the bottom. Sometimes a faded color that had become mostly white,
like it had been accidentally bleached. Sea green bleached. Never a sexy nightgown.

The palm tree curtains drop there.
They get the whole audience screaming.

Now, girls, dig it: *patriotic colors & orange frosted lipstick smeared on as blush.*

(Speaking of blush,)

In the late eighties/early nineties: a tea length, shapeless/drapey, scoop-neck dress with loose, short sleeves, the smudged, bright, "artsy" roses in the print emerging from a neutral background. Open-toed, bone-colored Naturalizer sandals.

Rose-colored lipstick. Rose-colored lipstick. Rose-colored lipstick. Rose-colored lipstick. Rose-colored lipstick. Rose-colored lipstick.

Dangling earrings.

BLUSHING HOLLERING LIKE AVOIDING AN AFTERNOON OF AVOIDING YOUR MA'S QUESTIONS

Drusilla won't stand for the hands-on-hips ironing the gum-popping charm the sex smell rubbed so hot on your lips and thumbs you can barely stand it thing
Drusilla is absolute Georgia O'Keefe and the walkways outside of the Louvre and fossil fossil fern flung fish the ocean the yarrow in a vase, like this, though: VAHZ

WAIT UP, BITCH: if it's Drusilla poking around my redhot car-room
coming here all ordinary
for an interview with the queen
and for a puff of my stash,
then are there two Drusillas?

And who's feeding lines today?

And then now soon yesterday it's obvious:
Drusilla *is* two
Giselle and Griselda are sobbing over some tabloids
all of them fly girls
all them in husband-y t-shirts threadbare on the nipples

Drusilla sleeps on a motorcycle and chokes on her lollipop.
Griselda writes quotes in a moldy steno notebook.
Giselle wears a prom dress in a gas station.
Drusilla please come to town,

Please admit something in front of the swollen applause.
Make it Burbank. Make it video. Make it fucked up.
WHOSE MOTHER? AND WHOSE LINE WAS THIS ONE?

I don't have my measuring rod with me, but I'm willing.

Drusilla, are you
willing
lonely
at the edge of town
in white and grey stripes, a peach-hued belt?

Last of all, there was the red dress.
It was taffeta and mid-length with a skirt of some slight volume
a tie at the waist
a skirt of some volume.
I was in love with that dress and when she wore it I felt jealousy and I wanted to be her.

Griselda, come to the very front of the stage for this part.
Giselle is behind, emerging from your mind.
Here, the curtains, the yellow satin, the stain of the falcon's eye close at hand at
shoulder-level at the masking tape X of here here step here
I was in love with that dress and when she wore it I felt jealousy and I wanted to be her.
I wanted to be her.

ARE YOU MORE THAN A MINIATURIST?
ARE YOU MORE THAN AN IMITATION?
ARE YOU MORE THAN A SLOB A COWARD CONSTANTLY
COMPARING YOUR SUFFERING AND YOUR CLOTHES TO OTHERS'?
DID WE BLOCK THIS SCENE RIGHT?

In this one, we need all three of them.

Pinch up your elbow skin, all of you.
Each one of you

under the bare light bulb
read from the podium. Read it breathy and last day of a murder scheme and
heart-wrenching as a crucifix under water.

She never wore contacts, just glasses large enough to hide her eye bags.

*I like to think that it's my mother's intense interest in clothing and makeup and nice
expensive clean looking clothes that accounts for my disinterest in clothes and makeup.*

She has for decades kept a style that has ease and manageability.

She doesn't like to brush her hair.

*I also am fond of memories of her with a red handkerchief folded into a triangle,
wrapped over her hair, and folded at the base of her skull behind the neck, which she
wore to dust or to work in the garden.*

She wore a turtleneck that had tiny holly leaves and berries printed on it.

Most days she wore an old sweatshirt and ripped jeans.

She had a lot of clothes, though she did not have any particular interest in fashion.

*I liked her closet, a walk-in with a light, a husband side, a wife side, the space long
enough for a person to sleep, though no one ever did that.*

*Once, she bought a legit ball gown from Goodwill to wear to her holiday work party.
It was black and satin(-y). There were ruffles. With some sequined silver lightning bolt
decorations near the shoulder pads.*

When my mom was promoted was also around that time in the early 90s when safari print bullshit was everywhere and I remember that she had a blouse with some strange khaki mixture of broad leaves, zebra print, and tigers that I was jealous of. She would pair it with a long, wide khaki skirt and wide-strapped sandals. Magical.

Winged. Puffy. Crispy. Charlie's Angels, but lobbed.

There have not been many days in my mother's life that she hasn't dried her hair with a hair dryer and a round brush.

She permed her hair when I was very small, but then I remember it being feathered so that it framed her face very well.

Mostly she wore shorts or pants, t-shirts from races or club events.

HOW DOES THE SELF
THE SELF INHABITING THE PERFORMANCE
KNOW HOW TO DRESS   THE LEAKAGE?

& HOW DOES IT DO WITH SHORTER FORMS?

Griselda and Giselle run to Drusilla's open bloody arms.
The stage is set as a charming garden.
Cartoon-character bed sheets blow on the line.

GET IN YOUR CAGE BABY.

   I wanted to be her.
This is PRECISELY how I have always operated.

Come on now a confession.

I like empty public spaces on holiday mornings.
I like pawnshops and poorly kept offices.
I like pop culture representations of Happenings.
I am a slob.

What I do is miniatures.
I have wanted to *be* every single girl ever.
I consume everything so awfully so ruthlessly so routinely.
I don't even know what else there is.
He says please come to see me I say no you come home.
It's a movie a play it's my bed.

Ma, baby, Baby, Daddy:
I cannot afford to lick my stories off some dead mountain.
You can reach me here in the back bedroom. Telephone cord anklets.
A rueful rashy twisting of the lips. I say DARLING and I say a malady of daisies.
I say it sleeping coughing coughing on a dick I say it all morning on coffee cups.

Here's the thing:
The theater must get very hot here.
The place has got to simply rot.

on

I showed my dad my Tori Amos cassette tape in the car.
I was probably going to run away with an old man who had money.
I was a high-rise lifeguard in a cute bikini and pale blue nail polish
and I was living inside of F. Scott Fitzgerald.
She would put her pantyhose on first, in the bedroom, in front of the dresser, which was
wide and low and had a mirror.

I have since very early childhood experienced some delight in the

you-know-who
gaze. The *his*
gaze *I could see her*

pubic hair pressing against the nylon.
I knew I would never run away with an old man.
I knew I was at my very core a coward.
Then, she would put her shaping briefs on, over the pantyhose,
pull them above her navel.
This arrangement would help keep the pantyhose from sliding down.
I remember using cover-up on my terrible teenager skin.
I remember with some degree of disgust my teenager body, the smells of my
perfumes and lips glossed to sticky pink, and sweat.
I know that polyester dresses and jackets take a lady's BO.

I know this from falling into my grandma's basement closets, where she kept her
decades of clothes. I would let my body drop into them, mimicking a grief scene
I'd witnessed on a Sunday night made-for-TV movie.

It seems like *Women on the Verge of a Nervous Breakdown.*
But it's not at all; that's just memory-holes.
She would bend forward when she put her bra on
so that her breasts would fall into the bra cups;
then stand up and adjust.
Her bra was the same stiff, serious beige as the briefs and I was a high-rise lifeguard
in a cute bikini
and pale blue nail polish.
She would apply Estee Lauder perfume,
aiming the spray toward her chest, then toward her crotch.

notes &
texts of
influence

Amy Winehouse's persona and posture and clothes in the video for "Fuck Me Pumps"

Andrea Rexilius's kindly introducing me to Surrealist parlor games

Anne Boyer's *Garments Against Women*

Anthony Barrett's *Agrippina: Sex, Power, and Politics in the Early Empire*

Clive Barker's stories' grotesqueries (and the film *Nightbreed*)

CAN YOU RECALL ONE OF YOUR MOTHER'S OUTFITS FROM
WHEN YOU WERE A CHILD?

Elaine Kahn's *Women in Public*

Elena Ferrante's Neapolitan Novels

Emily Greenquist's performances in the video-project *Romero*

Harmony Korine's *SPRING BREAKERS*

Jessica Johnson's description of the television program *Weeds*: "mom crack"

WHAT FASHION/ACCESSORY/MAKEUP TICK OR TRICK DID
YOUR MOTHER HAVE/USE TO FEEL HER BEST? OR RATHER:
WHAT IS YOUR OBSERVATION OF SUCH?

Johannes Göransson's *Haute Surveillance*

Julie Carr's *Objects from a Borrowed Confession*

Lana Del Rey's nightgown in "High by the Beach"

Louise Sorenson-Cronk's dream/nightmare of finding princess dresses stuffed into corners of a scary room

NEIU's English 384, 235, and 101 students' openness

IN WHAT GARMENTS DID YOUR MOTHER SLEEP WHEN YOU LAST LIVED WITH HER?

Netflix's *Hot Girls Wanted*

Nikki Wallschlaeger's *I HATE TELLING YOU HOW I REALLY FEEL*

Philip Sorenson's *Men's Fashions*

Plays Inverse's mission, especially in the form of Meg Whiteford's *The Shapes We Make with Our Bodies*

Rihanna's persona and hair in "Needed Me"

HOW WOULD YOU DESCRIBE YOUR MOTHER'S HAIR (FROM ANY ERA)?

Sandra Doller's *Leave Your Body Behind*

Susan Sontag's *Against Interpretation*

Suzanne Scanlon's *Her Thirty-Seventh Year, An Index*

Tan Lin's *Seven Controlled Vocabularies and Obituary 2004. The Joy of Cooking: [AIRPORT NOVEL MUSICAL POEM PAINTING FILM PHOTO HALLUCINATION LANDSCAPE]*

Taschen's collection of old issues of *Exotique*

Fashion reports in "who's chirping yer hand?" come from email responses to interview questions. The respondents are: Lina David, Jessica Johnson, Megan Martin, Daniela Olszewska, Christine Simokaitis, Katie Sorenson, Carleen Tibbetts, Sara Wainscott, Della Watson.

The extended fashion report in "on" comes from Christine Simokaitis.

CHENILLE

My Darius is holding a recording device to a doorway and drinking a glass of milk with icecubes in it.

I *wish* I could experience time outside of this dollhouse.

It must be simply grand.

But vast. Un-/dis-curated.
I won't ever
act disloyally on this, my latter, premise.

Ever.

I'm much too cowardly & he too unsettled.

We devour wills in its devour.

friends in sea-green blouses with scalloped collars & in a canoe

a bicycle in lace and blood

a cook named Sailor

the crisp existential rot of telegrams

the swampy gaps between memory and self and family

a beg of a blade

Jupiter sick with its gas

The story is   You can feel a snake two rooms away
a parlor away

at your neck

a teen's necklace

with its serpentine cursive that spells
Murder & Romance

but I
can't help it

from two rooms away

(I pretend that) my boyfriend was wearing eyeliner in those days. I remember a secondhand navy blue rain jacket and this one day when I got cut early at work and came home to an empty apartment and put on rose-scented lotion and

took a walk in that coat.

I could still go out into the neighborhood then. We both did. Read the papers. Rolled cigarettes. Strummed a few sad tunes over and over. Fell down drunk in front of the TV.

I am a vapor of everything I anticipate.

He
is blue ghost gas floating over the birdbath.

He is prone to compulsions
prone to

spider fingers all around the bedpost
illness as weather
garden dominion compulsions
the tin & twee & shameful mole-faced cup
of Shirley Jackson of
British psychedelia
of poison   mushroom   sister clocks,

(and how we have loved those)

He is prone
to watching
a gray bloated body with rainbow string bikini
ribboning it across it:

No matter his agitation, whatever you tell me, doctor, no matter, no matter

he is
the mirror tiger of my *favorite* times.
I tinker quietly around his sleeping body

just to sniff out
a fool screaming girl haunted house mimic,
to use it

to admit,
so awfully,

that I've always believed *feeling itself* to be unworthy of speech
—for myself and for others;

to marshal enough emotion
to parade it in language
to make the transmission worth it
seems simply outrageous to me
makes me just sick

I'm so sorry.
I have many faces,
and most of them are utterly cold.

The things I give to him during his dream time.
The way I drag ass to a patchouli lagoon. Wish radio backwards.
They're gonna make you wish you never came to my room.

We could still go out of the house then.

We could go.

Ten times slow mo walking through the Plaza de Santo Domingo
pencil skirt

I'm hooked on the notion of my own arm trailing beyond

as I pass through the tissue of membrane of precipice,

right there in the plaza in one world,
but one arm behind me, hanging onto/in the other world

& I grip him bitterly and tenderly at once,

It is always in heroic terms.
It is always winter.
It is bad wounds on the feet.
A bucket of cheap cookies.
He sleeps on and on.

I knew before
that to be woken from his dreams

would *ill* him. Fever-scarf.

I knew that
before.

I knew he was a planet.
Rubied.
Dollared.
A dead branch fulla dead birds and his tarot cards flipping
just as the window opens
just like that.

Cedar star,
doomed face, queen face, knight, toil, his face. The window the card.
Opens. He hollers his gaze.

Finish porcelain the garden. Shuffle the deck.

Home is the work/theater.

Home red chair burns the unicorn the vomit the old confetti.

Home is the only other world.

a howling Lazarus of an event

our Bauhaus Baby

the only rather there
only to rather wren split

to hold one another in perpetual, enclosing,
insect-trauma-escaping embrace
anyway

I'll be in in a bit

The impossibility of the stairs meeting us is like a play.

Sorrowful rabbit man inside of interchangeable pieces of doo-wop.

I imagine snails and rain
running across all of our conversations.
Afternoon repeated over and over on a psychedelic album.

Oh, Darius.
He & I. You & I.

The window the card.
The window the card.

Claustrophobia like Virginia Woolf.
Agoraphobia
opens a market to shame.
The tension essential

between the two. And a bedspread furthermore.

little stripe of neon nail polish blown wild
and Darius huffs on his sick
while our girl
acorn-print curtains swaying no

telephone call had a good laugh *a real good laugh*

but then the room rewrites his paranoia
like nothing you've ever seen
like parabasis and getting super high in the morning
murmuring up the silky obvious

Throw daddy details.

Though axing drear, a hard gentleman.

I could cut your sea gown curse
whole
for all of us.

are wings temporal are hunches vulturous
green plastic sandals
did it feel horrid

a single spooky eye peeking out through chiffon
contemptuously rolling about

and Noreen hopping away from the glistening pool of it, terrified

swan lions in stone
on the river

all animals howl up
to the *before*
the soft common is not at all

Darius, Noreen, rowing along
it skull it now woman it

In small neat ears, I ply a tacky melody: "Love's My Beating."
Like a rock-full, they're down. This is what I mean by the silky obvious.

If I picture him, it is this: his blue eyes, eyeglasses, naked, sipping water before coming to bed, stoned, red eyes, closed eyes, the smell of our unclean sheets and unwashed hair.

What gossamer is this we've doused into.
What eggshells typed against.
What small handwriting as vandalism.

Dust in his lump the kind of solitary pleasure.
Of this.

It is this
the how quickly of this

how we spend and spend
all the final layers of lipstick.

A polaroid teardrop.
A chanting in the yellow brown bramble
and harpsichord-y chirping types outside the corner store.

What you see is what you get.

For me, Ancient Times
are a bunch of stage shadows pushing me around & under apocalyptic
constellation maps.

He's more bodily. He grips heat teeth, feels the world as it truly is.
Noreen follows us room to room.

I worry that I am better at daily acts of sacrifice and martyrdom than
acting right in crisis.

I wring my bloody rags and rage.

From Neon Pearl: "You can hear your dream scream."
From Zoe Skoulding: "I don't represent places but I make poems as places where
I can exist, temporarily."

Aesthetic fetish and a funny glare at the video-hole

Darius huffs on his sick

I flip cards to the tune of the swirling cherry pies in his eyes

Noreen in a dirty white undershirt

Bird flashcards. A 1970s edition of the board game Memory. I flip the cards

Darius, do you remember when apron strings pulled and dropped into a book
and coins fell out and it was yesterday. And a fortune teller examined our
wedding rings in x-rays in her den. And our child sprang
right from the kill circle, in a hula hoop and
dressed full as pout
in Queen Anne's Lace?

The ways that people live. The investigation of the temporal *nasty*.

A bureau casts a shadow of a ghoul and we all avoid that room after dinner.

Start again inside of dry ice.
Chase a hallucination of a red scarf.
Darius, Noreen, and I.
Could there be a way of perceiving time
that is not bound to the dolls.
Could there ever be a gaze that isn't miniature, and wine-ish in its lens.

No.
I don't think so. Recording equipment times out

then

feel another person in writing/reading

a familiar bulge from under a piece of rubber

Darius what. How it is to feel you in your writing in my writing.

It could not get
more miniature than this.

I remember what kind of lady I am was in my cluttered chambers in narration of breed brood.

Now stretch that chamber light
into neon time
why don't you.

With a small stiff yarn whorled into your ear,
      who's your Phyllis Diller?
With all others, an icy layer of film between.
With Darius,
            dramatic musical ampersands
            ice bells in milk
            the familiar from earlier
            imprinted upon the ice
            our hands able to melt through
            the various vagues.

I'm spilling pearly bath beads here, Darius.

It's the how-yearns
that all those Leonard Cohen songs used to give me.

Sometimes, as a lady in my home,
I feel my cheekbones sweep into relief
against the décor
and

aglow with the narcotic panic of having had a premonition of his death, a car crash sound at the window, say, the phone's long ringing unanswered, perhaps, she'd run back and forth and between the front apartment windows and the bathroom mirror in an intricate touch-tarot of fortunetelling. By the time he'd have returned to the building, she'd have collapsed in theatrical anguish, having quickly turned the torso of him in her mind to face its inevitable culpability; *he was to blame* for the touch-tarot's read.

In an episode of *Wonder Years*, the mom and dad are engaged in a long-ish fight, which, we are to assume, is bound with the socio-cultural-historical conditions of the moment, a kind of (1960s) nostalgia that posits the utter violence as orange framed screens *juxtaposed* against all else, i.e. domestic life. (I've often enjoyed thinking of *era* in this way, even as I note the lies that buttress such a thing.) The mom and dad are fighting. The TV is showing war's bodies. The girl is rebelling. The middle class belts have been tightened. The fires seem to be burning right outside the door. The mom accidentally cuts herself with a kitchen knife, while washing the dishes, angrily. I think. Then the dad comes in and helps. They make up through a wound.

The cut skin is a walk through the fight.
They make up through a wound.
They make up over bloody skin.

As a child of parents whose fighting was a kind of stable backdrop to the all else, the scene appealed to me.

Darius says that I do not know how to have a fight.
I'm a door slammer, not a lover.

What could possibly be more delicious than saying something true and not true at the same time?

A particularly beautiful child that Noreen. Particularly.

And the lamb-worm sucks on a grass.

I am constantly pretending something. I don't mean in the obvious ways we must all do—work, parenting, social occasions; I mean: I'm always in my own aesthetics, to a fault, I think, to

the feeling of scrubbing the *burnt* of a sauce pan

the friction-y caressing of Noreen's dirty hands

haunted house pleasure a million times over

Darius's poems stuck in my head like a hot teenage summer

Darius's favorite songs my favorite songs

smoking pot like a hot teenage summer

all three of us hot in our hot apartment and playing songs

Noreen's drawings: touch-tarot

pancake dinner: all of the moons lined up for our pleasure lined up like a car over a cliff

Translation of any sort makes a bizarre and impossible and gaping hole, forces a
cave-collapse-storm where there is no weather. Family makes a hole, too.
The leap across: home. Done to me.

Mei-mei Berssenbrugge: "Time is ethos, as if we're engendered by our manner in
it, not required to be in ourselves."

In silk pajamas
in the garden Katherine Hepburn Myrna Loy forced onto my/her body of mask-y
vines
Noreen handling acid vials with lovely velvet fingers
a piglet in ice teeth chattering in a background song

Darius
Darius

in the kitchen Darius's police scanner goin' all evening
Darius
two cans of Hamms

he's in a mood

Noreen is writing inside my mouth
is the girl trap tonight

& you know what I load braids around how you sweet-voiced dawn that one time

I don't know how to explain what I mean other than to say I truly enjoy bougee
images from catalogues, and music/voiceover montage-letter-reading-scenes,
and that it turns out that it's true that ten years twenty years baby time toddler
time sunscreen rubbed on sand sticking to it hot walks to playgrounds and fixing
snacks
and then pouring wine glasses all summer evening
all of it is nothing

it is really truly nothing
and I hate trying to negotiate lived time and thought time
and most of it is spent unshowered and anxious and not doing anything nothing

Darius, what *is* wrong with me?

I cannot stand this constant circling to nothing strand

I am false

a false strand holding tideback a bundle of clichés, eight is a zero with a belt on,
infinity, etc., etc., our girl is growing like a

blah blah blah

In an alliance training session at work, after we are prompted to share a hidden
part of our identities, a woman whom I know only from her face says that she
had a child and this child died and she is alone in her knowing that she is a
mother

and this secret makes me want to die
writing this makes me want to die

I used to leave I left the house I am shopping doing errands I am being a lady in institutional bathrooms and Carly Simon fashions I was pretending this though

At home: Noreen, Darius, Noreen

Darius,

Everything leaks
from home
and like it's coming right into my purse like I packed it in the morning with my lunch.

I am on the bus and I want horribly to see Noreen
I am on the bus and thinking of Noreen's childish hedonism and how
she might she
be bound in compulsive preservationist tendencies as a system by which to stave off loss and thus maintain those hedonistic doorways. Keep the line open, so to speak.
My own trinkets and collections and my way of straightening the apartment over itself over its own hoarded-ness bear this out.

the hunger blue
a girl with a seahorse dress
copper circle on her ear

us three settled into the theater of home
I on the bus
us three settled into my purse
hello there

Nodding off in front of a comicbook robin stretched across several panels,
Darius upgazes me in my lake.

I am completely desired and completely alien
I have dragged my child along my knee while tracing letters on my knee
I have felt final skin in the tall grass of pretend

yellow spilled across
the soft-makingness

A butterfly woman covered in mud and wheezing at our back door. The
dissolving of the whole scene into this one itch I have always got:

dusky kitchen time, summer evening feels, a lace blouse or a pretty silver
bracelet, a lady singer coming out of a box, this era's family hunkered down into
lightness and air and a swaying curtain

That is not even it.
I don't know how to tell you even the simplest thing.

a sailor twenty-two oceans away
my wearing eyeliner the tissue of that

Can I just say that choosing you was one real good move.
Can we agree to the grim dish of our girl.

The membrane, I guess, *is* just parabasis, a river of selves whispering in the night
/ a sound-shaped river of Noreen's playing
through the non-dolled rooms.

what kind is I

my

family makes hole family is a translation afterall after what

I do not know if others prefer constraint as I do.
In all settings in which I operate, I choose not to choose.

This is to leave left compulsive and hedonistic a system.
I avoid losses by not keeping the keep of doors.

When I am outside,
I am still the one with Darius and Noreen but also pleased that I am different.

I am now buzzing and clammy from having tried to competently use my
Spanish to help a woman at the bus stop.

I am eating a sandwich at my desk.

I am naked in the locker room for a very short time, quickly pulling my swimsuit
over what I perceive to be the wobbly grey boulder of my ass.

I am swimming laps so fast because of flippers I received for my birthday. I feel
as water.

I am afraid of being perceived as uncaring when I stop to chat with a co-worker.

I am turning on Midori Takada's *Through the Looking Glass* to feel spooked in my
office.

I am looking at my mess of paper, books, pens, old greeting cards, candy
wrappers, half clean napkins, notes I wrote to myself.

I am sending messages.

I am offering warm greetings to people in the hallways and I am genuine in this,
but it absolutely exhausts me.

When I am at work, I can keep count more easily on the books I want to read.

At home, I make a wet ghost of the harm I do to others & I sleep on the damp.
With Darius sleeptalking next to me, sleeptalking like a demonic whisper
voiceover in all of my favorite movies all at once.

Sometimes my parents would fight so hard that my brother and I would run upstairs and our dog's ears would go back as if she had gotten in trouble for something and we'd hear the clanging and yelling, not entirely upsetting, soothing almost, the familiar *river of it*,

but once my parents were fighting on Christmas Eve and my father said he was leaving, a threat rarely uttered,

and because it'd been years since we'd heard this threat, and because it'd been in a different home we'd last heard this threat, and because he'd settled into a kind of weirdly peaceful domestic presence with all of us, reading his mass market fantasy and sci-fi paperbacks in his underpants and slippers at 6:45, right after dinner, after we'd all chowed down in front of *Wheel of Fortune*,

this threat on Christmas Eve seemed real & I sobbed in the bathroom & my father came in to tell me it was all just talk, never going to happen, and I don't think I even knew what I would have actually wanted, except, perhaps, no change, let nothing change,

I cannot bear
domestic re-order

I just can't figure it

Sibylle Baier: "Tonight when I came home from work/ there he unforeseen changed in the lazy chair."

Marguerite Duras via translator Barbara Bray: "As the mother had the same fear about the father—that without her he'd disappear—they were always alone together a la casa in the afternoon, obliged in a way to keep watch on each other. Though they probably weren't aware of it."

Without me Darius will disappear without him I
Noreen both renders us
and disappears us

Darius utters/writes: "We disappears."
This is real.
And not.

Darius mutters: "And not."

Today Noreen is two months away from turning six and she plays at being a
baby, gets out her baby doll supplies in order to use them as her own props, sits
folded into a doll stroller, sits laughing and whining in a secondhand dress, with
no underwear, sucking an old pacifier that I'd stored in her doll things.

I am reading about conjoined twins in Yugoslavia in 1986.

And not.

Noreen: "Baby me."

Today Noreen is almost six and pretending to be a baby.

She lays flat on our bed, atop a ripped Raggedy Ann blanket from my own
childhood.

She pretends to need a diaper change.

She acts hurt when I won't play.

Within ten minutes, the props are re-appropriated.

There is a baby school in the dining room now.

I am reading about the conjoined twins, how they bathe.

The babies all have their own beds. Noreen says some of them will need to listen
very carefully.

influences/
sources

Abigail Zimmer's *child in a winter house brightening*
Amanda Goldblatt (conversations and writings)
Amina Cain's *Creature*
Angel Olsen's body of work
Bridget St John's *Ask Me No Questions* and *Songs for the Gentle Man*
Currently and Emotion: Translations (ed. Sophie Collins)
Dolores Dorante's / translator Jen Hofer's *Style*
Gabriella Cohen's *Full Closure and No Details*
Grey Gardens (1975)
Grouper's *Dragging a Dead Deer Up a Hill*
Helene Cixous's / translators Sarah Cornell, Deborah Jenson, Ann Liddle, Susan
Sellers's "Coming to Writing"
Helen Humphrey's *The Frozen Thames*
Jasmine Dreame Wagner's *On a Clear Day*
Jay Besemer's *Crybaby City*
Jennifer Nelson's *Civilization Makes Me Lonely*
Julia Jacklin's *Don't Let the Kids Win*
Kenneth Anger's body of work
Lidija Dimkovska's / translator Christina E. Kramer's *A Spare Life*
Louise Sorenson-Cronk
Marguerite Duras' / translator Barbara Bray's *The Lover* and *Summer Rain*
Mei-mei Berssenbrugge's "I Love Morning"
Midori Takada's *Through the Looking Glass*
Nathalie Leger's / translators Natasha Lehrer and Cecile Menon's *Suite for Barbara Loden*
Neon Pearl's *1967 Recordings*
Nikki Wallschlaeger's *Crawlspace*
Philip Sorenson
Rachel Cusk's *A Life's Work* and *Outline*
Rihanna's *ANTI*
Shirley Jackson's *We Have Always Lived in the Castle*
Sibylle Baier's *Colour Green*
Tan Lin's *Insomnia and the Aunt*

acknowledgements

Thank you, Loulou, for the many ripe and startling ideas that you give me.

No reading, thinking, writing I do can ever happen without help from my family: Anne Zielenski Fleming, Ed Fleming, Louise Sorenson-Cronk, Nick Cronk, and Philip Sorenson. Much of my work, too, relies on nourishment from my NEIU students.

When I conceived of the concept of a "womonster," I had not yet read Jay Besemer's *The Ways of the Monster*. Later on, I did read it. And I read his note about the complexities of using "monster" metaphors at this moment, and now I am indebted to his ideas, and oh how wonderful that poetry time-loops all reading and thinking and writing.

Thank you Meg Forajter and Christian Peet; really, really: thank you.

Thank you to these spaces, where parts of these poems appeared: *Best American Experimental Poetry Digital Edition, Burning House Press, Columbia Poetry Review* blog, *Datableed, Iowa Review* blog, *La Vague, Make Magazine*.

about the author

Olivia Cronk is the author of *Louise and Louise and Louise* (The Lettered Streets Press, 2016) and *Skin Horse* (Action Books, 2012). With Philip Sorenson, she edits *The Journal Petra*.

TARPAULIN SKY PRESS

exquisite imagination ... (**Publishers Weekly** "**Best Books 2018**") warped from one world to another (**The Nation**); beautifully startling and fucked and funny and tender and sad and putrid and glitter-covered all at once. (**VICE**); simultaneously metaphysical and visceral ... scary, sexual, intellectually disarming (**Huffington Post**); only becomes more surreal (**NPR Books**); proves indie presses deserve your attention (**BuzzFeed News**); hallucinatory ... trance-inducing (**Publishers Weekly** "**Best Summer Reads**"); wholly new (**Iowa Review**); language dissolves into stream-of-consanguinity post-surrealism and then resolves into a plot again (**Harriet, The Poetry Foundation**); horrifying and humbling in their imaginative precision (**The Rumpus**); a world of wounded voices (**Hyperallergic**); riotous, rapturous, and radical (**LA Review of Books**); unapologetic work, so bitch and bad-ass (**VIDA**); Visceral Surrealism (**Fanzine**); as savagely anti-idealist as Burroughs or Guyotat or Ballard (**Entropy**); both devastating and uncomfortably enjoyable (**American Book Review**); consistently inventive (**TriQuarterly**); highly rewarding (**The Stranger**); feels like coming (**Maudlin House**); breakneck prose harnesses the throbbing pulse of language itself (**Publishers Weekly**); an orgy ... at once sexy and scientifically compelling (**The Rumpus**); dark, multivalent, genre-bending ... unrelenting, grotesque beauty (Publishers Weekly); futile, sad, and beautiful (**NewPages**); refreshingly eccentric (**The Review of Contemporary Fiction**); a kind of nut job's notebook (**Publishers Weekly**); thought-provoking, inspired and unexpected. Highly recommended (**After Ellen**)

MORE FROM TS PRESS >>

REBECCA BROWN
NOT HEAVEN, SOMEWHERE ELSE

If heaven is somewhere, it isn't with us, but somewhere we want to get — a state, a place, a turning to home. Novel- and essayist Rebecca Brown's thirteenth book is narrative cycle that revamps old fairy tales, movies, and myths, as it leads the reader from darkness to light, from harshness to love, from where we are to where we might go.

PRAISE FOR *NOT HEAVEN, SOMEWHERE ELSE*: "Aside from 'genius,' the other word I would use to describe Rebecca Brown is 'elemental'.... She's a genius at the invisible forces that bind words together.... It feels dangerous and exciting, like if she puts her big brain to it long enough, she could completely rewrite the story of who we are." (PAUL CONSTANT, *SEATTLE REVIEW OF BOOKS*) "Satisfied a desire for moral discussion I didn't even know I had.... Highly recommended and highly rewarding." (RICH SMITH, *THE STRANGER*) PRAISE FOR REBECCA BROWN: "Strips her language of convention to lay bare the ferocious rituals of love and need." (*THE NEW YORK TIMES*) "One of the few truly original modern lesbian writers, one who constantly pushes both her own boundaries and those of her readers." (*SAN FRANCISCO CHRONICLE*) "Watch for her books and hunt down her short stories." (DOROTHY ALLISON) "America's only real rock 'n' roll schoolteacher." (THURSTON MOORE, SONIC YOUTH)

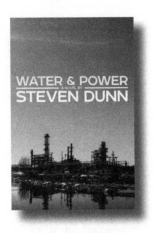

STEVEN DUNN
WATER & POWER

SPD Fiction Bestseller
Featured at *Buzzfeed News*:
"Books That Prove Indie Presses Deserve Your Attention"

Navy veteran Steven Dunn's second novel, *water & power*, plunges into military culture and engages with perceptions of heroism and terrorism. In this shifting landscape, deployments are feared, absurd bureaucracy is normalized, and service members are consecrated. *water & power* is a collage of voices, documents, and critical explorations that disrupt the usual frequency channels of military narratives. "Traversing both horror and humor, Dunn imbues his prose with the kind of duality that is hard to achieve, but pays off." (**WENDY J. FOX, *BUZZFEED NEWS***) "Dunn's remarkable talent for storytelling collapses the boundaries between poetry and prose, memoir and fiction." (**NIKKI WALLSCHLAEGER**) "Captures the difficult, funny, abject, exhilarating, heartbreaking and maddening aspects of Navy life, both on and off duty. Read this book and understand the veterans in your life better, understand the aggressive disconnection the armed forces demands, and retain a much clearer picture of the people who wear the uniform in America's name." (**KHADIJAH QUEEN**)

JENNIFER S. CHENG
MOON: LETTERS, MAPS, POEMS

Co-winner, Tarpaulin Sky Book Award, chosen by Bhanu Kapil
Publishers Weekly, Starred Review
SPD Poetry Bestseller
Nominated for the PEN American Open Book Award

Mixing fable and fact, extraordinary and ordinary, Jennifer S. Cheng's hybrid collection, *Moon: Letters, Maps, Poems*, draws on various Chinese mythologies about women, particularly that of Chang'E (the Lady in the Moon), uncovering the shadow stories of our myths. "Exhilarating ... An alt-epic for the 21st century ... Visionary ... Rich and glorious." (**PUBLISHERS WEEKLY STARRED REVIEW**) "If reading is a form of pilgrimage, then Cheng gives us its charnel ground events, animal conversions, guiding figures and elemental life." (**BHANU KAPIL**) "Each of the voices in Jennifer S. Cheng's *Moon* speaks as if she's 'the last girl on earth.' ... With curiosity and attention, *Moon* shines its light on inquiry as art, asking as making. In the tradition of Fanny Howe's poetics of bewilderment, Cheng gives us a poetics of possibility." (**JENNIFER TSENG**) "Cheng's newest poetry collection bravely tests language and the beautiful boundaries of body and geography ... A rich and deeply satisfying read." (**AIMEE NEZHUKUMATATHIL**)

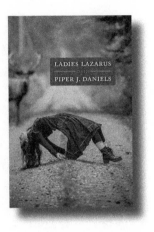

PIPER J. DANIELS
LADIES LAZARUS

Co-winner, Tarpaulin Sky Book Award
Nominated for the PEN/Diamonstein-Spielvogel Award
for the Art of the Essay

Equal parts séance, polemic, and love letter, Piper J. Daniels's *Ladies Lazarus* examines evangelical upbringing, sexual trauma, queer identity, and mental illness with a raw intensity that moves between venom and grace. Fueled by wanderlust, Daniels travels the country, unearthing the voices of forgotten women. Girls and ghosts speak freely, murdered women serve as mentors, and those who've languished in unmarked graves convert their names to psalms. At every turn, Daniels invites the reader to engage, not in the soothing narrative of healing, but in the literal and metaphorical dynamism of death and resurrection. "Beautifully written collection of 11 lyric essays ... Daniels emerges as an empowering and noteworthy voice." (*PUBLISHERS WEEKLY*) "*Ladies Lazarus* is the best debut I've read in a long time. Daniels has resurrected the personal essay and what it is and what it can do." (JENNY BOULLY) "An extremely intelligent, impressively understated, and achingly powerful work." (DAVID SHIELDS) "A siren song from planet woman, a love letter from the body, a resistance narrative against the dark." (LIDIA YUKNAVITCH)

STEVEN DUNN
POTTED MEAT

Co-winner, Tarpaulin Sky Book Award
Shortlist, *Granta*'s "Best of Young American Novelists"
Finalist, Colorado Book Award
SPD Fiction Bestseller

Set in a decaying town in West Virginia, Steven Dunn's debut novel, *Potted Meat*, follows a boy into adolescence as he struggles with abuse, poverty, alcoholism, and racial tensions. A meditation on trauma and the ways in which a person might surivive, if not thrive, *Potted Meat* examines the fear, power, and vulnerability of storytelling itself. "101 pages of miniature texts that keep tapping the nails in, over and over, while speaking as clearly and directly as you could ask.... Bone Thugs, underage drinking, alienation, death, love, Bob Ross, dreams of blood.... Flooded with power." **(BLAKE BUTLER, *VICE MAGAZINE*)** "Full of wonder and silence and beauty and strangeness and ugliness and sadness.... This book needs to be read." **(LAIRD HUNT)** "A visceral intervention across the surface of language, simultaneously cutting to its depths, to change the world.... I feel grateful to be alive during the time in which Steven Dunn writes books." **(SELAH SATERSTROM)**

ELIZABETH HALL
I HAVE DEVOTED MY LIFE TO THE CLITORIS

Co-winner, Tarpaulin Sky Book Award
Finalist, Lambda Literary Award for Bisexual Nonfiction
SPD Nonfiction Bestseller

Debut author Elizabeth Hall set out to read everything that has been written about the clitoris. The result is "Freud, terra cotta cunts, hyenas, anatomists, and Acker, mixed with a certain slant of light on a windowsill and a leg thrown open invite us. Bawdy and beautiful." (WENDY C. ORTIZ). "An orgy of information ... rendered with graceful care, delivering in small bites an investigation of the clit that is simultaneously a meditation on the myriad ways in which smallness hides power." (*THE RUMPUS*) "Marvelously researched and sculpted.... bulleted points rat-tat-tatting the patriarchy, strobing with pleasure." (DODIE BELLAMY) "Philosophers and theorists have always asked what the body is—Hall just goes further than the classical ideal of the male body, beyond the woman as a vessel or victim, past genre as gender, to the clitoris. And we should follow her." (*KENYON REVIEW*) "Gorgeous little book about a gorgeous little organ.... The 'tender button' finally gets its due." (JANET SARBANES) "You will learn and laugh . . . . God this book is glorious." (SUZANNE SCANLON)

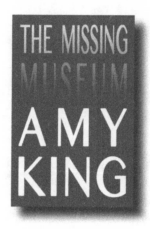

AMY KING
THE MISSING MUSEUM

Co-winner, Tarpaulin Sky Book Award
SPD Poetry Bestseller

Nothing that is complicated may ever be simplified, but rather catalogued, cherished, exposed. *The Missing Museum* spans art, physics & the spiritual, including poems that converse with the sublime and ethereal. They act through ekphrasis, apostrophe & alchemical conjuring. They amass, pile, and occasionally flatten as matter is beaten into text. Here is a kind of directory of the world as it rushes into extinction, in order to preserve and transform it at once. "'Understanding' is not a part of the book's project, but rather a condition that one must move through like a person hurriedly moving through a museum." (*PUBLISHERS WEEKLY*) "Women's National Book Association Award-winner Amy King balances passages that can prompt head-scratching wonder with a direct fusillade of shouty caps.... You're not just seeing through her eyes but, perhaps more importantly, breathing through her lungs." (*LAMBDA LITERARY*) "A visceral stunner ... and an instruction manual.... King's archival work testifies to the power—however obscured by the daily noise of our historical moment—of art, of the possibility for artists to legislate the world." (*KENYON REVIEW*)

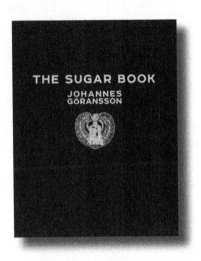

JOHANNES GÖRANSSON
THE SUGAR BOOK

SPD Poetry Bestseller

Johannes Göransson's *The Sugar Book* marks the author's third title with TS Press, following his acclaimed *Haute Surveillance* and *entrance to a colonial pageant in which we all begin to intricate*. "Doubling down on his trademark misanthropic imagery amid a pageantry of the unpleasant, Johannes Göransson strolls through a violent Los Angeles in this hybrid of prose and verse.... The motifs are plentiful and varied ... pubic hair, Orpheus, law, pigs, disease, Francesca Woodman ... and the speaker's hunger for cocaine and copulation..... Fans of Göransson's distorted poetics will find this a productive addition to his body of work". **(PUBLISHERS WEEKLY)** "Sends its message like a mail train. Visceral Surrealism. His end game is an exit wound." **(FANZINE)** "As savagely anti-idealist as Burroughs or Guyotat or Ballard. Like those writers, he has no interest in assuring the reader that she or he lives, along with the poet, on the right side of history." **(ENTROPY MAGAZINE)** "Convulses wildly like an animal that has eaten the poem's interior and exterior all together with silver." **(KIM HYESOON)** "'I make a language out of the bleed-through.' Göransson sure as fuck does. These poems made me cry. So sad and anxious and genius and glarey bright." **(REBECCA LOUDON)**

AARON APPS
INTERSEX

"Favorite Nonfiction of 2015," Dennis Cooper
SPD Bestseller and Staff Pick

Intersexed author Aaron Apps's hybrid-genre memoir adopts and upends historical descriptors of hermaphroditic bodies such as "imposter," "sexual pervert," "freak of nature," and "unfortunate monstrosity," tracing the author's own monstrous sex as it perversely intertwines with gender expectations and medical discourse. "Graphic vignettes involving live alligators, diarrhea in department store bathrooms, domesticity, dissected animals, and the medicalization of sex.... Unafraid of failure and therefore willing to employ risk as a model for confronting violence, living with it, learning from it." (AMERICAN BOOK REVIEW) "I felt this book in the middle of my own body. Like the best kind of memoir, Apps brings a reader close to an experience of life that is both 'unattainable' and attentive to 'what will emerge from things.' In doing so, he has written a book that bursts from its very frame." (BHANU KAPIL)

Excerpts from *Intersex* were nominated for a Pushcart Prize by *Carolina Quarterly*, and appear in *Best American Essays 2014*.

CLAIRE DONATO
BURIAL

A debut novella that slays even seasoned readers. Set in the mind of a narrator who is grieving the loss of her father, who conflates her hotel room with the morgue, and who encounters characters that may not exist, *Burial* is a little story about an immeasurable black hole; an elegy in prose at once lyrical and intelligent, with no small amount of rot and vomit and ghosts. "Poetic, trance-inducing language turns a reckoning with the confusion of mortality into readerly joy at the sensuality of living." (*PUBLISHERS WEEKLY* "BEST SUMMER READS") "A dark, multivalent, genre-bending book.... Unrelenting, grotesque beauty an exhaustive recursive obsession about the unburiability of the dead, and the incomprehensibility of death." (*PUBLISHERS WEEKLY* STARRED REVIEW) "Dense, potent language captures that sense of the unreal that, for a time, pulls people in mourning to feel closer to the dead than the living.... Sartlingly original and effective." (*MINNEAPOLIS STAR-TRIBUNE*) "A grief-dream, an attempt to un-sew pain from experience and to reveal it in language." (*HTML GIANT*) "A full and vibrant illustration of the restless turns of a mind undergoing trauma.... Donato makes and unmakes the world with words, and what is left shimmers with pain and delight." (BRIAN EVENSON) "A gorgeous fugue, an unforgettable progression, a telling I cannot shake." (HEATHER CHRISTLE) "Claire Donato's assured and poetic debut augurs a promising career." (BENJAMIN MOSER)

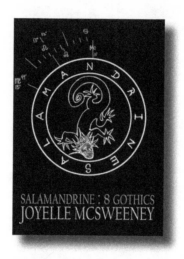

JOYELLE MCSWEENEY
SALAMANDRINE: 8 GOTHICS

Following poet and playwright Joyelle McSweeney's acclaimed novels
Flet, from Fence Books, and *Nylund, The Sarcographer*, from Tarpaulin
Sky Press, comes a collection of shorter prose texts by McSweeney,
Salamandrine: 8 Gothics, perhaps better described as a series of formal/
generic lenses refracting the dread and isolation of contemporary life
and producing a distorted, attenuated, spasmatic experience of time,
as accompanies motherhood. "Vertiginous.... Denying the reader any
orienting poles for the projected reality.... McSweeney's breakneck prose
harnesses the throbbing pulse of language itself." (*PUBLISHERS WEEKLY*)
"Biological, morbid, fanatic, surreal, McSweeney's impulses are to go
to the rhetoric of the maternity mythos by evoking the spooky, sinuous
syntaxes of the gothic and the cleverly constructed political allegory. At
its core is the proposition that writing the mother-body is a viscid cage
match with language and politics in a declining age.... This collection
is the sexy teleological apocrypha of motherhood literature, a siren song
for those mothers 'with no soul to photograph.'" (*THE BROOKLYN RAIL*)
"Language commits incest with itself.... Sounds repeat, replicate, and
mutate in her sentences, monstrous sentences of aural inbreeding and
consangeous consonants, strung out and spinning like the dirtiest
double-helix, dizzy with disease...." (*QUARTERLY WEST*)

JENNY BOULLY
NOT MERELY BECAUSE OF THE UNKNOWN THAT WAS STALKING TOWARD THEM

"This is undoubtedly the contemporary re-treatment that Peter Pan deserves.... Simultaneously metaphysical and visceral, these addresses from Wendy to Peter in lyric prose are scary, sexual, and intellectually disarming." (*HUFFINGTON POST*) In her second SPD Bestseller from Tarpaulin Sky Press, *not merely because of the unknown that was stalking toward them*, Jenny Boully presents a "deliciously creepy" swan song from Wendy Darling to Peter Pan, as Boully reads between the lines of J. M. Barrie's *Peter and Wendy* and emerges with the darker underside, with sinister and subversive places. *not merely because of the unknown* explores, in dreamy and dark prose, how we love, how we pine away, and how we never stop loving and pining away. "To delve into Boully's work is to dive with faith from the plank — to jump, with hope and belief and a wish to see what the author has given us: a fresh, imaginative look at a tale as ageless as Peter himself." (*BOOKSLUT*) "Jenny Boully is a deeply weird writer— in the best way." (**ANDER MONSON**)

MORE FICTION, NONFICTION, POETRY & HYBRID TEXTS FROM TARPAULIN SKY PRESS

FULL-LENGTH BOOKS

Jenny Boully, *[one love affair]**

Ana Božičević, *Stars of the Night Commute*

Traci O. Connor, *Recipes for Endangered Species*

Mark Cunningham, *Body Language*

Danielle Dutton, *Attempts at a Life*

Sarah Goldstein, *Fables*

Johannes Göransson, *Entrance to a colonial pageant in which we all begin to intricate*

Johannes Göransson, *Haute Surveillance*

Noah Eli Gordon & Joshua Marie Wilkinson, *Figures for a Darkroom Voice*

Dana Green, *Sometimes the Air in the Room Goes Missing*

Gordon Massman, *The Essential Numbers 1991 - 2008*

Joyelle McSweeney, *Nylund, The Sarcographer*

Kim Parko, *The Grotesque Child*

Joanna Ruocco, *Man's Companions*

Kim Gek Lin Short, *The Bugging Watch & Other Exhibits*

Kim Gek Lin Short, *China Cowboy*

Shelly Taylor, *Black-Eyed Heifer*

Max Winter, *The Pictures*

David Wolach, *Hospitalogy*

Andrew Zornoza, *Where I Stay*

CHAPBOOKS

Sandy Florian, *32 Pedals and 47 Stops*
James Haug, *Scratch*
Claire Hero, *Dollyland*
Paula Koneazny, *Installation*
Paul McCormick, *The Exotic Moods of Les Baxter*
Teresa K. Miller, *Forever No Lo*
Jeanne Morel, *That Crossing Is Not Automatic*
Andrew Michael Roberts, *Give Up*
Brandon Shimoda, *The Inland Sea*
Chad Sweeney, *A Mirror to Shatter the Hammer*
Emily Toder, *Brushes With*

G.C. Waldrep, *One Way No Exit*

&

Tarpaulin Sky Literary Journal
in print and online

tarpaulinsky.com

CPSIA information can be obtained
at www.ICGtesting.com
Printed in the USA
FSHW012027300520

9 781939 460226